In the World, Not of the World

A collection of short verse
from a Latter Day Saint

*The greatest gift that God has given me is Shauna.
I write for you, my love.
I also give thanks to the Lord for giving me the inspiration.*

IN THE WORLD

In The World 6
Wisdom 7
The Runner 8, 9
Elusive Thoughts 10
Nagging Thoughts 11
Creative Thoughts 12
My Wandering Mind 13
Age 14
Fatigue 15
Deceit 16
Moving Lips 17
Corruption 18
Today's World 19
Ode To My Friend 20, 21
Burnt Cookies 22
Pushup Lizards 23
Roman Soldiers 24, 25
Writers Block 26
The Drum 27
Sacrifice 28
Honor 29
Rejection 30
Children 31
The Aborted 32
Depression 33
Consequences 34
Narcicissm 35
The Dog Who Wanted To Fly 36
Stuff 37
Rain 38
Pessimism 39
Hawaii 40
Locusts 41
Madness 42
Betrayal 43
The Fire 44, 45
Natalie Hates School 46

iii

NOT OF THE WORLD

Not of the World 48
Dirt 49
Listening 50
God's Grace 51
The Gift 52
Come Follow Him 53
Under Water 54
The Railing 55
The Lion Roared 56
The Chief Watchman 57
The Bully 58
The Teacher 59
The Lighthouse 60
Like a Wadi 61
Disciples 62
Eternal Love 63
Blessings 64
The Dance 65
The Dream 66
Alchemy 67
The Gathering 68
The Seeker 69
Freedom vs. Agency 70
Turn To God 71
But If Not 72
Choices 73
Good And Bad Thoughts 74
Trials 75
Truth 76
Prophets 77
Marriage in the Covenant 78
Agents or Objects 79
Illustrations 81, 82

In the World

In The World

*In the world
not of the world
is hard sometimes to be,
but I have to try
to be guided by
the holy trinity.*

Wisdom

I thought knowledge was the king,
And then one day I found,
That knowledge may be good to seek,
But wisdom wears the crown.

The Runner

The runner knelt down,
and awaited the sound
he would hear from the crack of the gun.

To his beating heart
the big race would soon start.
In his mind he had already won.

At the sound of the gun
all the racers did run
and the runner jumped out to a lead.

He breathed in the air,
with the wind in his hair,
as his feet began to pick up speed.

The first hurdle came,
then came more of the same,
he had sprinted ahead of them all.

He stumbled a bit
then a hurdle he hit
and it was a disastrous fall.

He sat there in shame,
and he could only blame
himself for the bad choice that he made.

As others passed by,
the downed runner did cry,
then an observer came to his aid.

He put down his cup,
to help the runner up
then he said, "Go continue the race."

The child shook his head,
his incentive was dead.
As he gazed into the kind man's face

He said , "I'm a disgrace
I will not even place
Or win the most coveted first prize."

The Observer smiled,
and he said "You're wrong child,
You will always win if you just rise."

Elusive Thoughts

There are days when my thoughts are great.
They will obey my beckoned call.
And some days they won't come at all.
My brain cells won't cooperate.

At least when my thoughts won't appear,
To show me what I want to say,
A dictionary shows the way.
Thank goodness it is always near.

Nagging Thoughts

I toss and turn, I cannot sleep.
Those nagging thoughts in my mind creep.
"Get out damned thoughts!" I want to cry,
But I'll awake my wife nearby.
And so I lie with open eyes,
'Til I can't fake it, then I rise.

Creative Thoughts

Creative thoughts are fun to think
And test my right brain's vision.
But sometimes it can be real hard
To come to a decision.

My Wandering Mind

When I am concentrating so
On something that I need to know,
I lose my focus then I find
I'm trapped inside my wandering mind.

Age

At first age comes like winter snow.
You wait and wait.
Then finally the day arrives
When flurry flakes fall from the skies.

But later age becomes a foe.
A dreaded date.
Then suddenly the day arrives
When no more flakes fall from the skies.

Fatigue

While I sit in the trench of repetition
Volleys of routine tasks zip past my head.
I struggle to pay attention.
My eyelids battle to stay open.
I want to scream but no sound escapes my mouth,
Only a rush of charging air.
Over and over like wave after wave of determined troops
Fatigue pounds me incessantly.
I must stay awake but my will weakens
with each minute that marches by.
I can't resist any longer. I give in. I close my eyes.
Waking with a start,
I find myself covered in the blood of discovery.
I have been taken prisoner by the enemy,
And fatigue has won the battle.

Deceit

He said he'd take away our fears
As we watched hopeful with our peers.
Some gave him support and their cheers
Rang in our ears, rang in our ears.

Now every night I go to sleep
Into my mind disturbed thoughts creep.
His promises he didn't keep.
Deceit runs deep, deceit runs deep.

Moving Lips

"If his lips are moving, he's telling a lie."
My sweet wife wants some to believe.
"I'm telling a story," I say with a wink.
"A lie's when you try to deceive."

Corruption

The news comes on and in my mind,
I dread to hear what's next.
I turn away, pick up the phone
and read a friendly text.

When I turn back I hear the man
on T.V. tell his tale
Of crooked politicians and
elitists dodging jail.

It seems one side has all the power
to bring their rivals down,
Accusing them of things they do.
Hypocrasy abounds.

The lies, deceptions that they speak,
I want to stand and scream.
It's almost like I'm living through
a twisted, dreadful dream.

And then wise counsel pricks my mind
To always trust the Lord.
The evil ones who seem to thrive
Will someday feel His sword.

Today's World

We're bombarded every day
with messages that often say,
Don't be content with what you have
Call now and buy this golden calf.
Our website you will surely find
a doodad that will blow your mind!
Or if it's pleasure you desire,
We'll really set your soul on fire.
We have the product that you need
So buy it now and feed our greed.
Our devious words you sure can trust
So order now, you really must!
And honesty, that's real passé
That concept is unknown today.
And if you doubt my words are true,
I'll find a way to cancel you.
You there, you must watch our show,
then like it and before you know,
We'll hook you then we'll reel you in,
Just like a fish, enjoy the sin.
And if we disagree with you,
We'll blame you for bad things we do.
We'll lie and cheat without a thought,
And keep on stealing 'til we're caught.
And even then we shall deny
The proof you see is just a lie.
And when you think it can't get worse,
A thief will say, "Give me your purse."

Ode To My Friend

A neighbor came to me one day and said I need your aid,
A big stray cat eats my cats' food and makes them sore afraid.
I know you have a love for cats and if you would be willing,
Please take him in and make him yours so I avoid his killing.

I told her I would do just that so he would have a home,
I'd feed him, groom him, show him love so he would cease to roam.
And so that day I saved his life to ease both of our minds.
Sometimes the clouds rain down on us and sometimes the sun shines.

The years went by through heat and cold and still he learned to thrive.
Being chased by dogs and fights with cats he managed to survive.
Through travels far in confined spaces he came through it well,
He learned to acclimate himself as far as I could tell.

And then one day a fire arose and we received the call,
Sometimes the sun shines down on us and sometimes rain does fall.
Another journey out of harm in one cramped little car.
We took all that we thought we should and then we traveled far.

A new home and a new beginning with help from above.
Our needs were met more than we'd hoped, we truly felt God's love.
Through all the changes we endured my friend came through it fine.
Sometimes the clouds rain down on us, sometimes the sun does shine.

All seemed to go well for a while until a dark cloud came,
And hovered over my sweet friend; he didn't seem the same.
No medicine would ease his pain nor food would satisfy,
There wasn't much that I could do except to sit and cry.

I couldn't let him suffer so I took him to the vet,
And asked him if a miracle could save my friend and yet,
I knew there were no miracles that could heal him and so,
I realized that maybe it was time to let him go.

I held my friend until he went into a peaceful sleep,
And my heart stopped when my friend's did, then I began to weep.
Sometimes the sun shines down on us and sometimes the rain falls.
All that we can hope for is we'll be ready when God calls.

I miss you Mr. Stinky

Burnt Cookies

I crave some cookies,
I mentioned one night,
If you make then I'll bake,
They'll turn out just right.
My wife made the batter,
I put on a sheet.
Then into the oven,
It's going to be sweet.
I dialed in the timer,
And sauntered on out,
Then after some time passed,
I heard my wife shout.
"The cookies are burnt,
That is your fault," she cried.
I had lost track of time, so
I sat down and sighed.
I looked at my wife,
She was ready to bawl.
"If we eat them," she said,
"We'll need Pepto Bismol."
"Wait," I declared, "I know,
We'll take them next door.
Along with some Pepto,
That's what friends are for.
(Note: We actually did this)

Pushup Lizards

I looked out the window and what did I see
A lizard on the wall in front of me.
Spring had brought me such an odd surprise;
A lizard doing pushups right before my eyes.
I remembered Army days that weren't so sweet;
A drill instructor's whistle he would often tweet.
It was so long ago, when I seemed to be,
Like the push-up lizard right in front of me.

Roman Soldiers

Tramp, tramp, tramp, the steady sound
Of hob-nailed boots on rocky ground.
The rhythm of the drums keep time,
While soldiers follow them behind.

Some pray to gods, "Mars smile on me,
So I'll be strong like horses hooves."
Some hope they will not turn and flee
Like frightened children chased by wolves.

The soldiers keep a watchful eye
On their surroundings they pass by.
The trees could hide a stealthy foe,
Armed with a lance or with a bow.

Then, when the men feel all worn out,
Their leader sees they need a rest.
"Troop halt, break ranks, relax," he shouts.
The soldiers seek the shade that's best.

They take long drinks of water, warm,
Unlike cool water from a storm.
But it still quenches throats so parched,
After a hundred leagues they've marched.

*And when all have received their rest
They form ranks and prepare to move.
Some are examples of Rome's best,
And some men have a lot to prove.*

*Then tramp, tramp, tramp the steady sound
Of hob-nailed boots on dampened ground.
And once again the men march on.
Another day is nearly gone.*

*They finally reach their place to camp
And set up goat skin tents for shade.
The ground is somewhat cold and damp,
Conditions that a spring rain made.*

*Then all must sleep except for those
Who keep a watchful eye for foes.
When morning comes, the soldiers rise
To breezy winds and somber skies.*

*Then they form battle lines and wait.
Each man is anxious to engage,
And find out what will be his fate.
Inside they feel a burning rage.*

*Some are on foot, some are on steed,
The business of death will proceed.
The enemy cannot avoid
Their destiny, they'll be destroyed.*

Writer's Block

I sat at my desk, it was really a mess,
I looked at the wall clock and sighed.
I stared at the screen, hoping brilliance I'd glean
From my brain cells that haven't yet died.

"C'mon!" I exclaim, to my overworked brain,
As the tick-tocking blared from the clock.
But it was no use, I had run out of juice,
So I had to give in to the block.

The Drum

The drum beats steady as it goes,
Sometimes it's fast,
Sometimes it slows,
When it will stop, the drummer knows,
The drum beats steady as it goes.

Sacrifice

You answered your great country's call.
You knew the hallowed cost,
But still you went and gave your all
So freedom wasn't lost.

So raise a glass to those who fell,
To keep our country free,
Remember them who went through hell.
They died for you and me.

Honor

*There is no greater honor
than to live an honest life.
A man who's true to others,
God, his children, and his wife.*

Rejection

Rejection is a dreaded foe,
We all must endure now and then,
It teaches perserverance, though,
I would not call it my dear friend.

So don't give up I tell myself,
And keep on trying, you will see
Put those rejections on the shelf.
If it's God's will, he'll give to thee.

Children

They start out small and then grow tall,
The food they can consume.
School books, school clothes and lunches,
And they never clean their room.

Please close the door, mud on the floor,
You hope someday they'd learn.
That money doesn't grow on trees,
They think it's just to burn.

Then comes the day you shout Hooray!
It's time for them to go.
And then the realization hits,
You'll really miss them so.

The Aborted

Silent voices cry in pain,
"We want to live," they say,
But evil ones ignore the pleas
And take their lives away.

Depression

Depression reared its ugly head
As I lay resting on my bed.
I told myself "Why should I rise
When all my choices I despise.

The world kept crashing down on me,
No respite came to set me free.
It seemed no matter what I tried,
My sadness made me want to hide.

I had to let go of that rope
That robbed me of my faith and hope.
I said, "O Jesus, hear my prayer,
And help me through this dark despair.

Then came a light from up above
That bathed me in God's perfect love.
A new resolve then filled my heart
And so I made a brand new start.

Consequences

I do without thinking sometimes,
How my doing affects those around me.
I do without caring sometimes,
How my doing affects those around me.

I must think, when I do, about others.
What I do affects not only me.
I must care, when I do, about others.
What I do affects not only me.

I say without thinking sometimes,
How my saying affects those around me.
I say without caring sometimes,
How my saying affects those around me.

I must think, when I say, about others.
What I say affects not only me.
I must care, when I say, about others.
What I say affects not only me.

What I do always has consequences.
It can be for the good or the bad.
What I say always has consequences.
It can be for the good or the bad.

Narcissism

Fall down on bended knee.
I deserve praise you see.
I'm a celebrity
So you must indulge me.

Self-absorption can be
Egocentricity.
I abhor modesty
And despise empathy.

So don't you come to me
Dreaded humility.
There is no room for thee
I embrace vanity.

The Dog That Wanted To Fly

There once was a dog
That wanted to fly.
In his heart he thought he was a bird.

Then that foolish dog
Would jump up so high,
Until one day he received the word.

You can't be a bird,
You just don't have wings,
In the air you won't get very far.

We'd all like to be
A myriad of things,
Just be satisfied with who you are.

Stuff

*We all
must have stuff
there's no doubt.
But what stuff is needed
or what stuff is wanted?
How much stuff
can we do
without?*

Rain

Rain can bring life,
Rain can bring death,
Rain has a dual personality,
But both kinds can take away breath.

Pessimism

"It's going to get worse,"
I can hear myself say,
That's when I should think of
a much brighter day.

The negative thoughts
That sometimes fill my mind,
I must replace with good,
And leave them behind.

But it's hard to do
When bad habits won't die.
But it can be done if
I consciously try.

Hawaii

Sun, tikis, palm trees, leis, and sea,
The warm and sandy beach,
Souvenirs, shells, aloha shirts
Were all within my reach.
It was my lucky fortune
To be sent to paradise,
When other places at the time
Were not nearly as nice.
I had three years with Uncle Sam
And I would spend them there.
Sometimes my duty was hard but
I didn't really care.
I surfed and took up volleyball
And got a wicked tan.
When I took leaves my mother thought
I was a different man.
Then came the day I had to say
Aloha to it all.
Then I flew to an air force base
And gave my mom a call.
She picked me up and asked me if
I had some kind of plan.
Soon after I found my own place
And my new life began.

Locusts

Here come the locusts,
They cover the ground,
And assault the air
With their horrific sound.

They spoil all that's good,
They leave such a mess,
Care just for themselves,
Put the world in distress.

We need more seagulls,
To come to our aid,
And maybe the locusts
Will then be afraid.

Madness

It seems the world has gone quite mad.
Our leaders seem to fan the flames.
They turn all that's good into bad,
And play their corrupt insane games.

Their main goal seems just to divide,
And put us at each other's throat.
Our dangerous streets make us hide,
While those with security gloat.

When will all this craziness end?
When will we abrogate the fear?
It's time for a rescuing friend.
O Jesus when will you appear?

Betrayal

I feel like I betrayed
A friend's trust that I made.
My motives were quite pure
But my friend wasn't sure.

My actions caused him pain
And now guilt racks my brain.
I plead with God and say
Please take this guilt away.

My friend is gone and I
Can't tell him now just why
I did what I thought best
And now my friend's at rest.

Perhaps there'll come a day
When my guilt fades away.
But now I fear I've made
Him feel he was betrayed.

The Fire

That day is burned into my mind,
The day disaster came.
We woke up to a morning that
Just didn't seem the same.
The sky was dark instead of light
And then I got the call.
Our son said, "Dad, evacuate
Or you will lose it all.
A fire is heading straight for you,
No time to hesitate,
Pack up your car, head down the hill
Before it is too late."
We went through rooms like hurricanes,
Collecting what we could,
Then stuffed the car with all the things
We thought we really should.
While countless cars crawled down the hill
A yellow tinted sky
Hung over our ill-fated town
Just like a Devil's eye.
Losing so many treasured things
Was hard for some to bear.
Not even cities down below
Escaped the smoke-filled air.

Some thought the fire was minor and
They could return to see
That all was well but all was not,
From tree to burning tree.
The people who remained behind
And thought they would be spared,
Became the victims of the fire
And paid for what they dared.
When it was over we went back
To see a smouldering heap,
In place of where our house once stood.
All we could do was weep.
The first thing entering in my mind:
"What are we going to do?"
Then a warmth swept over me
And that is when I knew
We'd be okay and God would see
Us through this grave ordeal.
It took some time and patience
For the feelings to fully heal.
And now we're in another home
We felt God led us to.
The blessings He has given us
Are more than just a few.

Natalie Hates School

So, Natalie
Why can't you see
That school is just
Another key,
Which lets you
Unlock the right door,
That opens to
prospects galore.
So study hard
And you will see
A bold new world
For Natalie.

Not of the World

Not of The World

We often hear, "Be in the world, not of it."
What does that really mean?
Reject the filth and the lies the world spews out,
And keep your spirit clean.

Dirt

Dirt can deprive
Dirt can ruin
Dirt can destroy
Dirt can stain
Dirt causes grief
Dirt causes despair
Dirt causes misery
Dirt causes pain
Dirt cannot bring joy
Dirt cannot bring peace
Dirt cannot uplift
Dirt cannot win
Dirt is corrupt
Dirt is thoughtless
Dirt is greedy
Dirt is sin

Listening

When we pray we should take time to listen
If we want our dear Savior to hear us.
Listening can allow us to hear him.

Listening is a trait we should treasure,
The prophet has told us repeatedly.
When we pray we should take time to listen.

It's a good habit for all to follow,
And can help us all grow spiritually,
If we want our dear Savior to hear us

Then we must concentrate for our minds to
Be in tune with the Savior's advice.
Listening can allow us to hear him.

God's Grace

God's grace is like the sea,
It's always there for me,
If I obey his will
The waves will remain still.

But if I choose to sin,
The waves come crashing in,
If I don't turn around,
My spirit just might drown.

The Gift

Great is a gift
God's given me
He let me come
On earth to be
A mortal man
Among the rest
To see if I
Could pass the test
And so I came
Down from above
To obey Him
And learn to love
But now my life
Is almost done
And when I stand
Before God's Son
I know my soul
Will feel a lift
For Jesus is
The greatest gift.

Come Follow Him

Long ago a star shone bright
And bathed a babe in radiant light.
Three wise men saw the star that night
That seemed to say, "Come follow Him."

The babe grew and became a man.
An integral part of God's plan.
And so his ministry began
With simple words, "Come follow Him."

Then people came to hear him preach,
And many of them he did reach,
And many of them he did teach,
When apostles said, "Come follow Him."

And like the Savior I can be,
A better pathway I can see,
If I just listen to His plea
When he entreats, "Come follow Me."

Under Water

Is my faith under water?
I hope not.
Am I sinking and holding my breath?

Is the light shining down
growing weaker?
Will a watery grave be my death?

Have I done all I can to
find Jesus?
In my words, thoughts, and deeds every day?

If I haven't then God
throw a lifebuoy,
And help this willing soul swim the way.

The Railing

There is a railing that we all can grasp hold of
If we're willing.
It is filling
Up our souls with the stories of prophets and kings,
And creations
That formed nations.
Perhaps you know of another name which it's called:
The iron rod,
The word of God.

The Lion Roared

The lion roared,
It was the Lord
Who did chastise his people of old.

God's chosen ones strayed,
And very few prayed,
And their hearts became hardened and cold.

Wooden idols they made,
And with harlots they laid,
They had wounded their God to the core.

So when they wouldn't repent,
A great destruction he sent,
And the people heard the lion roar.

The Chief Watchman

The chief watchman stands on his watchtower
To warn us when enemies come,
But if we ignore his grave warnings,
And to his alerts we are numb,

Then we must accept what befalls us,
The watchman cannot share the blame.
The watchman is blameless forever,
For Jesus the Christ is his name.

The Bully

Do what I say or I'll hurt you,
The bully exclaims to his prey,
But it will hurt more if I listen
To what the bully has to say.

A Savior has come to my rescue,
To provide me his advocacy.
If I will allow him to save me
From the bully, then I can be free.

The Teacher

The teacher shows,
The teacher tells.
His wisdom shines
Like pearly shells.

If I ignore him
I'll pay the price.
He is the teacher,
He is the Christ.

The Lighthouse

At times we lose our way
Like lost ships in the night.
To avoid all the rocks,
We must seek out the light.

The keeper will always
Keep the clear beacon bright,
To show us all the way
When the dark shrouds our sight.

So come to the lighthouse,
Feel the warmth of the light,
Leave the tempests behind,
And you will choose the right.

Like a Wadi

Is my devotion to God like a wadi?
Is my soul dry and barely alive,
Like the sun beating down in a valley,
That is waiting for rain to revive?

Then I must be like the rainy season,
Where good deeds are like rain from the sky,
Then a river of blessings will follow,
That will fill my devotion when dry.

Disciples

The boy received his call
to be a true disciple of the Lord
as he opened the official letter.

A girl reeived her call
to be a true disciple of the Lord
as she opened the official letter.

Just two of many called
by the Lord through his appointed leaders
who are also His disciples as well.

We can be disciples
and spread light in a world in which Satan
is trying his best to lead us to hell.

We don't require a call
or an official letter from the Church
sent by the Lord's true chosen apostles.

We just need the desire
to share the gospel with those we contact
and we will also be His disciples.

Eternal Love

A greater love there cannot be
than that which lasts eternally.
Not shackled by the worldly rhyme
Nor hindered by the sands of time.

Blessings

A modest home, conveniences,
and transportation too,
A mind that can create and think
of countless things to do.

Good friends and neighbors near to me
who smile when I come by,
The mountains, lakes, the forests,
and the canyon lands nearby.

A family who cares for me,
a gospel that brings joy,
A loving God in Heaven
who knows every girl and boy.

The Dance

"The dance's length, no one can tell,
So strum the lyre and ring the bell.
And while we hope the dance extends,
Musicians choose when the music ends.
(From the novel-The Praetorian and the Emperor's List)

The Dream

I had a dream the other night
A dark room I was in
I felt like I was put there
For some unrepentant sin.

I cried aloud, "Why am I here?
What covenant have I broke?"
A light came shining down on me,
And then a soft voice spoke.

He called me by my name and said,
"If covenants you break,"
You'll lose all that you hold dear, and
Your glory I will take."

I woke up shaking like a child
That's been out in the cold,
Without a coat or jacket
Or a blanket I could hold.

I knew then that I must fulfill
Each promise that I make.
So I can walk in sunlight
With the Lord and not forsake.

Alchemy

I am lead but of the fold,
I pray the Lord turn me to gold.
I vow to be a loyal son
And shall submit, Thy will be done.

A lot of work's ahead of me,
But there's a light that I can see.
If I am faithful in the fold,
Then someday I will shine like gold.

The Gathering

There was a lone fish in the sea,
Then two gathered, then gathered three,
Then soon gathered four and many fish more,
They were happy as any could be.

Then one day the happiness left,
And all the fish were quite bereft.
Some went to the shallows, some went to the deep,
They just couldn't join in one school.
Then all of their promises they couldn't keep,
Put them in a dark, dismal pool.

A fisherman then came along
And gathered the fish in a throng,
He said follow me, and I'm sure you will see,
This true fisherman won't steer you wrong.

There were many fish in the sea,
The fisherman gathered with glee.
But still quite a few had washed up on the shore,
They just couldn't join in one school.
And others who thought that they wanted much more,
Wound up in the dark, dismal pool.

The Seeker

I am the seeker
I seek out the light
I live for the day
And not for the night

I seek out knowledge
I seek out wisdom
That draws me closer
To Father's kingdom

I am the seeker
Of truth and the right
The Savior guides me
When I keep him in sight

Freedom vs. Agency

You take away my agency
the young boy told his dad.
With all the rules you put on me
You're making me quite sad.

His dad replied, "Your agency
Can't be removed by me.
It is a gift God gives you that
Allows you to be free,

To choose the right or wrong each day
When choices you must make.
So always choose the right, my son,
And never God forsake.

Your freedom is what I control.
In my house I've the say.
Even God has given to us
His rules we should obey."

Then his son smiled and said to him,
"Thanks, now I understand,
You've built our house upon the rock
And not upon the sand."

Turn To God

Some find it odd
to turn to God.
the world they know
deletes him, so

they turn away
and seek out sin,
forsake to pray
and revel in

the pleasures of
desire not love,
and other things
contentment brings,

but God will wait
for their return,
it's not too late
for them to turn.

But if Not

Long ago a king's edict said
Forsake your God or you'll be dead.
Three brave young men chose to defy
The king's command, they'd rather die.

They knew the furnace was their fate,
And felt their harm, God would abate.
But if not, all would still be well,
T'was better than the fires of hell.

Then God smiled down on those three souls
And took the burning from the coals.
When all the people looked inside
They saw four men, no one had died.

So if dire threats in your life come
And circumstances look quite glum,
Jesus will pluck you from that limb,
But if not, you will be with Him.

Choices

Each day God has given me
another wondrous gift.
And each day Satan tells me
I should choose from God to drift.

Each day I can see the light
in all God blesses me.
And each day Satan whispers
that with him I can be free.

But Satan is a liar and his
only choice is sin.
So I choose God who someday
will allow me to come in.

Good and Bad Thoughts

The Savior says to think good thoughts
And feast upon his holy word.
Avoid all that corrupts and rots
Our testimony of the Lord.

But sometimes bad thoughts cause some doubt
And tempt me to partake of sin.
But with God's help I push them out
That's when I find real peace within.

Trials

"Why me, O Lord," I start to pray,
Please take this trial far away.
I'm sure my suffering is unique,
Urgent relief is what I seek.

And then the Lord smiles down on me,
My son be patient, you will see,
That trials are here and then they're gone,
It's always dark before the dawn.

I think of others down the line,
Whose trials have been much worse than mine.
My troubles aren't so bad I say,
I look to God and then I pray.
Forgive me for my selfish call.
The Savior's trials surpassed them all.

Truth

What is truth? Pilate once said,
Now some believe that truth is dead,
While others say our truth is right,
Your truth is wrong, give up the fight.

It doesn't matter what's your view,
It only matters what you do.
So look up to a higher sphere,
God's truth is all that matters here.

Prophets

Prophets, seers, and revelators are God's chosen ones,
Foreordained in heaven they are his appointed sons.
Favored daughters of our God can also join the sect,
All still have the option to accept or to reject.

For God gives us our agency and we still have a choice,
But Satan wanted selfishly to take away our voice.
So Jesus Christ stepped in and said,
"I'll do the Father's will."
God sent him down onto the earth, His kingdom to instill.

Christ's coming was foretold by men and women long before
He came to earth as they predicted, opening the door
To show the way, the truth, the light
so we can always know,
The path to take, the prophets testified of long ago.

Now many claim to speak for God and say,
"Come follow me."
Just put a dollar in my hand and I will pray for thee.
But money doesn't pick a prophet or can buy God's love.
The one God chooses only needs His guidance from above.

Marriage in the Covenant

Someone to share,
Someone to care,
We long to find the one.
And when we do,
We start a new,
The woman, man, and Son.

Agents and Objects

Are we God's agents or are we objects?
Do we act or are we acted upon?
When a call is given for service
Do we show up or are we gone?

Are we seeking to do good in the world?
Or just letting the chances pass us by.
Do those up in heaven smile on us
Or see our inaction and cry?

You can email Rod at: rod@rwarren.art and be put on his email list for upcoming projects and drawings for free books

Illustrations by Rod in his other books:
The Praetorian Trilogy

Illustrations by Rod in his other books: Who Let This Guy In The White House?

www.ingramcontent.com/pod-product-compliance
Lightning Source LLC
LaVergne TN
LVHW051035070526
838201LV00009B/201